SCIENTISTS
AT
WORK

Biologists
at Work

SIMONE PAYMENT

Britannica®
Educational Publishing

IN ASSOCIATION WITH

ROSEN
EDUCATIONAL SERVICES

Published in 2018 by Britannica Educational Publishing (a trademark of Encyclopædia Britannica, Inc.) in association with The Rosen Publishing Group, Inc.
29 East 21st Street, New York, NY 10010

Distributed exclusively by Rosen Publishing.
To see additional Britannica Educational Publishing titles, go to rosenpublishing.com.

First Edition

Britannica Educational Publishing
J.E. Luebering: Executive Director, Core Editorial
Mary Rose McCudden: Editor, Britannica Student Encyclopedia

Rosen Publishing
Nicholas Croce: Editor
Nelson Sá: Art Director
Nicole Russo-Duca: Designer
Cindy Reiman: Photography Manager
Nicole Baker: Photo Researcher

Library of Congress Cataloging-in-Publication Data

Names: Payment, Simone, author.
Title: Biologists at work / Simone Payment.
Description: New York : Britannica Educational Publishing in association with Rosen Educational Services, 2018. | Series: Scientists at work | Includes bibliographical references and index.
Identifiers: LCCN 2016058555| ISBN 9781680487510 (library bound : alk. paper)
| ISBN 9781680487497 (pbk. : alk. paper) | ISBN 9781680487503 (6-pack :alk. paper)
Subjects: LCSH: Biologists—Juvenile literature. | Biology—Vocational guidance—Juvenile literature.
Classification: LCC QH314 .P39 2017 | DDC 570.23—dc23
LC record available at https://lccn.loc.gov/2016058555

Manufactured in the United States of America

Photo credits: Cover, p. 1 © iStockphoto.com/sestovic; p. 4 © Radu Razvan/Fotolia; p. 5 Arun Roisri/Moment/ Getty Images; p. 6 In the collection of the Museo Nazionale Romano, Rome, public domain; p. 7 Hero Images/Getty Images; p. 8 © Flying Colours Ltd./Getty Images; p. 9 Walter Reed/U.S. Army; p. 10 Pakhnyushchy/Shutterstock. com; p. 11 Joel Sartore/National Geographic Image Collection/Getty Images; p. 12 Tim Roberts/Taxi/Getty Images; p. 13 Thomas Barwick/Iconica/Getty Images; p. 14 Karen Kasmauski/Corbis Documentary/Getty Images; p. 15 The zoology of the voyage of H.M.S. Beagle, under the command of Captain Fitzroy, R.N., during the years 1832 to 1836, Volume 2 (p. 320) by Charles Darwin (Smith Elder and Company, London, 1839); p. 16 © outdoorsman/Fotolia; p. 17 oBebee/Shutterstock.com; p. 18 Jeff Foott/Bruce Coleman Inc.; p. 19 Delmas Lehman/Shutterstock.com; p. 20 © Tommy Schultz/Fotolia; p. 21 Jeffery Rotman/Corbis Documentary/Getty Images; p. 22 aodaodaodaod/ Shutterstock.com; p. 23 PhotoObjects.net/Thinkstock; p. 24 Chase Dekker Wild-Life Images/Moment/Getty Images; p. 25 Oliver Born/Biosphoto/Getty Images; p. 26 © Michalis Palis/Fotolia; p. 27 Alan Kearney/Photolibrary/ Getty Images; p. 28 Keith Brofsky/UpperCut Images/Getty Images; p. 29 Hill Street Studios/Blend Images/Getty Images; interior pages background image Suwit Ngaokaew/Shutterstock.com.

Contents

The Many Jobs of Biologists

Biology is the study of living things. Biologists try to understand the natural world and the things that live in it. These things include plants, animals, fungi, protozoa, algae, bacteria, and viruses.

The study of biology covers many areas. It is usually divided into separate branches, or fields. Some biologists study anatomy, or the structure of living things. Some study ecology, or how organisms interact with their environment.

In addition to general fields, some branches of biology study

This biologist is using a microscope to examine a sample in the laboratory.

certain types of living things. Some biologists study large groups, such as all animals (zoology) or all plants (botany). Others study specific groups, such as mammals (mammalogy) or birds (ornithology).

Marine biologists study how many types of creatures interact in a specific environment—the ocean. Other biologists called paleontologists study creatures of the ancient past. Conservation biologists look to the future and how life forms interact with Earth's changing environment.

COMPARE AND CONTRAST

Which jobs in biology do you think are most similar? Which do you think are most different? Why?

Study of Biology in History

Aristotle studied anatomy and many other branches of biology in ancient Greece.

No one knows exactly when humans first began to study biology. Most biologists agree that it was thousands of years ago. Many of today's ideas started from the work of scientists who lived long ago.

For example, a Greek philosopher named Aristotle may have been one of the first people to study sea life. He lived from 384 BCE to 322 BCE. Aristotle also set up a system of classification to group animals into categories, or classes.

Early biologists did not have much equipment to help them in their studies.

Many improvements have been made to microscopes and other magnifying devices since they were first used.

They had to rely on information they could gather with their own senses. When biologists began using tools such as microscopes and binoculars, they were able to learn more about plants, animals, and the environment. For example, microscopes helped biologists study creatures that are too small to be seen with the eye alone.

THINK ABOUT IT

What other effects do you think the invention of the microscope had on the study of biology?

Anatomy

Anatomy is the study of the structures that make up the bodies of living things. Scientists learn about body structures mainly by dissecting, or cutting apart, bodies. They may dissect human or animal bodies, plants, or other life forms such as bacteria. Scientists identify the structures inside the life form and how they are put together.

Some biologists who study anatomy work in laboratories. They use microscopes to study tiny structures in the body, such as

This model of the human body has removable parts so that students can learn how the parts of the body work and fit together.

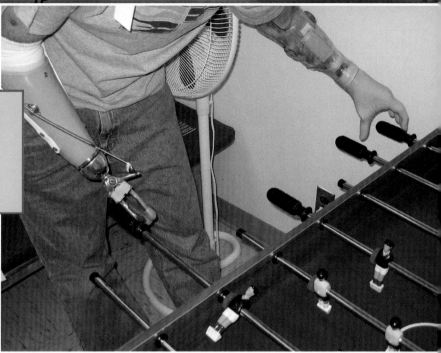

Anatomists design artificial limbs, such as these arms, to function the same way natural limbs do.

cells and their parts. Other anatomists study the way the parts of the body interact.

Some anatomists teach people who are studying to become doctors, nurses, dentists, or eye doctors about body structures. Anatomists also might do research or work for a company that designs artificial arms and legs, or hearing aids.

COMPARE AND CONTRAST

Which body parts might be similar or different among humans and other animals?

Ecology

Ecologists study the relationships between living things and their environments. Ecologists also study how living things use natural resources such as air, soil, and water to stay alive.

Some ecologists work in laboratories. Laboratory experiments allow ecologists to study things under controlled conditions. For instance, they can experiment to see how plants react to different amounts of light or water. This would be harder to do in nature, where weather and other natural conditions cannot be controlled.

However, many ecologists do work in natural, outdoor settings. They look

Ecologists may study how bees rely on flowers for food and how flowers rely on bees in order to reproduce.

This ecologist is looking for an endangered species of frog in a pond.

at all the different factors that affect **ecosystems**. Studies in the outdoors are useful because they show what is actually happening in the environment.

Ecologists also study how changes in the environment affect the survival of living things. For example, when pollution kills certain living things, the animals that feed on them may also die.

VOCABULARY

An **ecosystem** is all of the living and nonliving things in an area.

Botany

Botany is the study of plants. Scientists who work in the field of botany are called botanists.

Botany is important because people and animals depend on plants in many ways. People and animals get food and oxygen from plants. People also use plants to make clothing, building materials, chemicals, drugs, and many other things.

Some botanists discover new kinds of plants, name them, and classify them (group them with similar plants). Other botanists study the structure and form of plants.

Many botanists work as researchers.

Botanists use a variety of tools, such as tablet computers, to photograph and identify plants in the field.

These students are learning about plants and animals in a greenhouse.

Some researchers study plant diseases. Others experiment with plant chemicals. Others try to develop plants that are more useful to humans.

THINK ABOUT IT

Why does it help scientists to classify plants into groups?

Many botanists are interested in conservation. Some investigate the effects of pollution on plants. Others work to protect rare plants.

Zoology

Zoology is the study of animal life. Scientists who work in this field are called zoologists. They study all different kinds of animals, from tiny plankton to humans to giant whales.

Zoology is divided into many different areas. The name of each area is based on the group of animals being studied. For example, primatology is the study of primates.

Some zoologists examine animals' bodies and study how they live. They may answer questions about how the animals behave, how their bodies work, or how they live in their environment. Other zoologists study how animals have

Some zoologists study animals that live in zoos, such as this giant panda at the San Diego Zoo.

Charles Darwin studied hundreds of different birds and animals, including this bird, named the Darwin's rhea.

evolved, or changed, over time. One of the greatest zoologists was Charles Darwin. He developed the theory of **evolution**.

Some zoologists study animals that are extinct, or no longer living. They may examine the remains or traces of extinct animals that lived long ago.

VOCABULARY

Evolution is the theory that all the kinds of living things that exist today developed from earlier types.

Mammalogy

Mammalogy is a branch of zoology. Mammalogists study mammals. A mammal is an animal that breathes air, has a backbone, and grows hair at some point during its life. In addition, all female mammals have glands that can produce milk. Mammals are among the most intelligent of all living creatures.

Mammals include a wide variety of animals, from cats to humans to whales. There are about five thousand species, or kinds, of living mammal.

Mammalogists study behaviors of mammals, such as whales that leap out of the water.

Mammalogists may work in the field to study mammals in their natural environment.

Because there are so many different mammals, most mammalogists study a particular type. They may also study particular physical features and behaviors that help mammals survive.

Mammalogists often study living mammals in their natural environment. Other times they study mammals living in a zoo or a nature preserve. Mammalogists may also do research in laboratories.

THINK ABOUT IT

Mammalogists who study ocean mammals such as whales and dolphins face special challenges in their research. What are some of these challenges?

Ornithology

Ornithology is another branch of zoology. Ornithologists study what birds eat, where they build nests, where and how they fly, and many other things related to how they survive.

Early ornithologists could only study birds that they could easily see. After binoculars were invented, ornithologists could get a better look at birds and learn more about their habits. Ornithologists today use many types of technology, such as

Ornithologists who work in the field use tools such as binoculars to observe birds in their nests.

Birds often migrate in groups, including these snow geese flying over Pennsylvania.

satellite tracking, to study bird **migration**. They can also attach tiny radio transmitters to birds to track their flight.

Many ornithologists work in the field, studying a specific type or group of birds. They may travel to different locations to study birds as they migrate between their summer and winter homes. Other ornithologists work in laboratories to study bird anatomy or how chemicals or pesticides affect birds.

VOCABULARY

Migration is the regular movement from one location to another during the year that living things do for feeding or breeding purposes.

Marine Biology

Marine biology is the study of life in the oceans. Some marine biologists study one type of ocean creature, such as whales or turtles. Other marine biologists study how populations of sea creatures interact with one another to make up a community within a certain area of the ocean.

Some marine biologists work underwater, in submarines and other vehicles that can go deep into the ocean. Others work on land, studying marshes and other areas near the water's edge. Sometimes marine biologists work in laboratories

Marine biologists study sea life, such as this sea turtle swimming through a coral reef in the Pacific Ocean, surrounded by many other ocean creatures.

Some submarines are controlled from a ship in the water above, but others can carry marine biologists deep under water.

to investigate the contents of water samples or to examine microorganisms.

Marine biologists usually work in saltwater environments, such as oceans or the salt marshes near oceans. Freshwater biologists focus on freshwater environments, such as lakes, ponds, and streams.

COMPARE AND CONTRAST

What are some of the differences between what a freshwater biologist might study and what a marine biologist might study?

Paleontology

Paleontologists study the history of life on Earth. They study fossils, bones, and other evidence left behind by ancient plants and animals. Many people think paleontologists only study dinosaurs but that is not true (although some paleontologists do study dinosaurs).

Paleontologists often specialize in what they study. For example, paleobotanists study plant fossils. Vertebrate paleontologists study fossils of animals

Paleontologists often study fossils, such as this one of a fish. Fossils can be millions of years old.

that had backbones. Paleoecologists study the characteristics of environments in which ancient plants and animals lived.

When paleontologists are working to a dig up **fossils** at a site, they begin by using shovels and picks. When they get closer to the fossils, they begin using smaller and smaller tools. This way they do not damage the fossils when they are digging.

Sometimes, paleobotanists find fossils of plant life. Even a grain of pollen can give them information about ancient life.

VOCABULARY

Fossils are traces or prints of plant or animal remains from long ago that have been preserved in earth or rock.

Conservation Biology

Conservation biologists study how to protect things found in nature. They try to preserve natural resources, such as water, soil, minerals, wildlife, and forests, so that these resources will still be around in the future. Conservation biologists study how climate changes and how humans affect the variety of life that exists on Earth. They work to prevent the extinction of species, or types of living things.

Most branches of biology have been around for hundreds or even thousands of years. Conservation biology is a much newer branch of biology. It was formed after scientists became

Polar bears need sea ice to hunt seals. However, increasing temperatures on Earth are melting sea ice. This threatens the lives of polar bears.

aware of worldwide **extinction** and losses of species.

Conservation biologists perform field studies to count plant and animal populations in an environment. They also work in laboratories and use computer programs to make estimates about how climate changes are affecting plant and animal populations.

Attaching tracking bands on birds can help conservation biologists monitor and study the population of a species.

VOCABULARY

Extinction is when a species, or type, of living thing has completely died out.

25

Restoration Ecology

In the field of **restoration** ecology, scientists work to repair ecosystems that have been damaged by human actions or climate change. They study habitats that have been damaged or changed. For example, restoration ecologists might work in areas where there have been forest fires or hurricanes. Or they might work in areas where humans have cut down trees or caused the earth to erode.

Restoration ecologists think of ways to fix the environment. Then they make repairs. For example, they might replant grasses or trees in fire zones or on riverbanks. The roots of the plants can help

After a forest fire, restoration ecologists can help speed up the recovery of the damaged environment by planting certain plants.

keep the earth in place. The grasses can also help clean the water in rivers or marshes.

Climate change can affect animals, such as birds or insects, in a particular location. Restoration ecologists may also try to move the animals to a new area where the climate is better for their survival.

These ferns are growing in an area damaged by a fire in Yosemite National Park in California.

Studying for a Career as a Biologist

Biologists are making exciting new discoveries every day. New technology and equipment help biologists find new deep-sea animals or microscopic creatures.

Anyone can become a biologist. Biologists study math, science, and other subjects in school. Some biologists study drawing to record their findings in detailed illustrations. Others study writing and communication to explain their discoveries to other people.

Studying for a career in biology does not just take place in school. Anyone can

It's never too early to start studying for a career in biology. Visit your local museum to explore the wonders of the science.

Students interested in biology could take an after-school class at a museum or attend a science summer camp.

study plants in a backyard, or visit a museum to look at fossils, or go to a zoo to observe the similarities and differences that exist among various primates.

Biologists themselves have many differences. However, all share a common curiosity about how living things interact with one another and occupy our world.

THINK ABOUT IT

What are some things that you are studying now that could help prepare someone for a career in biology?

Glossary

ALGAE Living things (including seaweeds) that were once thought to be plants, but that do not produce seeds and are not divisible into roots, stems, and leaves.

BACTERIA Single-celled creatures that can be found in all natural environments.

BINOCULARS A hand-held device for seeing at a distance that is made up of two small telescopes.

CONSERVATION The protection of things found in nature.

ERODE To carry away bits of rock and earth from their original location.

EXPERIMENT A procedure done under controlled conditions to discover something or to test an idea.

FUNGI Simple living things, such as molds or mushrooms, that are neither plants nor animals and that must live on decaying matter, such as decomposing animals and plants.

HEARING AID An electronic device worn in a person's ear to make sounds louder so the person can hear better.

LABORATORY A place to do scientific tests and experiments.

MARSH An area of soft, wet land, usually overgrown with grasses and related plants.

MICROORGANISM Living things that are too small to be seen with the naked eye.

MICROSCOPE A device that magnifies tiny objects, or makes them look larger.

ORGANISM A living being made up of organs and able to carry on the activities of life, such as a person, animal, or plant.

PLANKTON Tiny living things that float and drift in the world's oceans and other bodies of water.

PRIMATE A group of mammals that includes humans, apes, monkeys, tarsiers, lemurs, and lorises.

PROTOZOA Any of a large group of single-celled animals that are mostly too small to be seen with the naked eye.

SENSE The ability to perceive sight, hearing, smell, touch, and taste.

SPECIES A category of living things that ranks below a genus, is made up of related individuals able to produce fertile offspring, and is identified by a two-part scientific name.

VIRUS Tiny particles that cause disease in people, animals, or plants.

For More Information

Fabiny, Sarah. *Who Was Rachel Carson?* New York, NY: Grosset & Dunlap, 2014.

Guillain, Charlotte. *Jobs if You Like Animals*. Chicago, IL: Heinemann Library, 2013.

Guillain, Charlotte. *Jobs if You Like Science*. Chicago, IL: Heinemann Library, 2013.

Kochanoff, Peggy. *Be a Pond Detective*. Halifax, NS: Nimbus Publishing, 2016.

Koontz, Robin. *Marine Biologists*. North Mankato, MN: Rourke Educational Media, 2016.

Morlock, Theresa. *Ecology*. New York, NY: PowerKids Press, 2017.

Websites

Because of the changing nature of internet links, Rosen Publishing has developed an online list of websites related to the subject of this book. This site is updated regularly. Please use this link to access the list:

http://www.rosenlinks.com/SAW/bio

Index